SEAN EDWARDS

AMERICAN
RESURRECTION

THE FAILURE

OF THE U.S. CONSTITUTION

AND THE REBIRTH OF A NATION

AMERICAN RESURRECTION

AMERICAN RESURRECTION

The Failure of the U.S. Constitution and
The Rebirth of A Nation

Designed by Sean Edwards
EdwardsPublishingHouse.com

Cover Design by Juan Lopez Design
JuanLopezDesign.net

Published in Spokane, Washington, by Edwards Publishing House

Edwards Publishing House
2910 E 57th Ave
Suite 5 #330
Spokane, WA 99223

ISBN-13: 978-0985771546
ISBN-10: 0985771542

Other Books by Sean Edwards:

The End of Days:
The Shocking Truth About The Times In Which We Live

Gay Marriage:
Why Conservative Christians Need To Support It

We Are The Danger:
A Christian's Call To End The War On Drugs

Table of Contents

About the Author

Sean Edwards was born in Knoxville, Tennessee. After moving between several locations within the United States, he landed in Spokane, Washington.

He graduated from Western Washington University with two Bachelor of Arts Degrees in History and Ancient Studies, and then attended the Bethel School of Supernatural Ministry in Redding, California.

Sean's passions include politics, economics, theology, eschatology, and the dynamics between the roles of government and faith.

Learn more about Sean Edwards at:

www.SeanEdwards.com.

Introduction

"Europe was created by history.
America was created by philosophy."

⁓ Attributed to Margaret Thatcher ⁓

The United States of America is a unique entity in the
world. This is not said out of clichéd patriotism, but
rooted in the United States' founding purpose. Every
other nation in history has existed because people
lived there and they needed a government. The U.S.
is different. It was born out of an idea. It was created
for a purpose. No other nation can say that.

Early Americans did not die for land, power, or
prestige. They did not go to war because of some
political game or spat between rulers. They went to
war over an idea that was so powerful, so dear, and
so precious to them that they shed their blood for it.
This should give us great cause for contemplation. Is

our patriotism today inspired by the same heartbeat of our founding generation? Or is it no different than the blind, tribal patriotism we have seen from the dawn of time?

I believe we have lost touch with our purpose and our identity as a nation, and it is time that we remember who we are.

The idea that turned the world upside down two hundred and fifty years ago is so radical and progressive that it can do it again today. Our forefathers only laid the foundation. We must build the rest.

Innocent Until Proven Guilty

I do not want to write another book that sparks violent debate. I want to engage people in a sensible discussion about the purpose of government and what it means for our everyday lives.

I value every person in this dialogue, no matter their party affiliation. I choose to believe that everyone in this discussion wants the best for our country. I refuse to believe that most people decide to run for office or become a political activist for nefarious reasons. I refuse to believe that they want to "wage war on the poor" or "destroy the constitution" or "send this country into bondage." That kind of language is flashy and eye-catching, but it casts people as simple caricatures with either halos or horns. It does not produce fruitful discussion, but rather hate and dissent.

We must also confront the assumptions that government is inherently evil, and that you can't trust politicians. These ideas have become so salient that they have made all attempts at a rational discussion almost impossible.

Government is not evil in its nature. It is a tool that society uses to harmonize life amongst its people. Just like any other tool, it exists without any moral predisposition. Someone can use it for evil, but someone else can also use it for good. It depends on who wields it.

Just as government isn't evil by nature, neither are politicians. There is no question that some individuals have violated the trust of the American people. But that does not mean that politicians en masse are not trustworthy. You do not condemn a whole group of people for the actions of a few. This is called bigotry and is akin to racism. Just as I cannot call all black people criminals, I cannot call all politicians liars. It is wrong to judge one individual by the actions of another.

Politicians and political activists are people. Few set out with a political agenda that says, "I'm going to screw the little guy." But this is, in essence, what many Americans believe. This assumption has seeped its way into almost every aspect of the political discussion. You will often hear people throwing around this joke,

"When can you tell that a politician is lying? When his lips are moving." We cannot allow this prejudice to continue–it has destroyed our ability to move forward.

Should we hold our elected officials accountable? Yes. Do some people seek power for their own personal gain at the expense of others? Yes. Does that mean we should operate from the assumption that all politicians cannot be trusted? No.

People are people. They have the capacity for evil, but they also have the capacity for good, and most choose to be good.

Let's enter this discussion assuming the best in people. Let's assume that people want to do the right thing, even if we don't agree with their ideas. Let's assume that people's motivations are innocent until proven guilty.

The Goal of this Book

It is my goal to illustrate just how radical the concept of liberty can be. I don't want to have a heady discussion about the purpose of government (though we will discuss it). There are plenty of books already written about that.

This book is on the power of inherent equality.

Most schools, both public and private, fail to teach the whole story as to why the colonies went to war.

The current curriculum castrates it and depicts a group of colonists that didn't want to pay their taxes. Taxes were not the issue.

Americans are not taught what it means to be American. Society has relegated the ideas behind the revolution to philosophers and historians – while the rest of us are left to repeat phrases and slogans without understanding their meaning.

I want to share these forgotten aspects of our nation with you.

The true implications of liberty, and what it means for us today, will challenge just about every perspective you have. It doesn't matter if you're liberal or conservative. The ideas that led to the Revolution will challenge some of your most cherished beliefs.

Yet, there comes a time when we must consider whether our ideals have affected the change we want to see. Friedrich Hayek said it best in his book *The Road to Serfdom*:

> "Is there a greater tragedy imaginable than that, in our endeavor to consciously shape our future in accordance with high ideals, we should in fact have unwittingly produced the very opposite of what we have been striving for?"[1]

---

1. F. A. Hayek, *The Road to Serfdom* (Routledge, London: The University of Chicago Press, 2007), 60.

Having your perspectives challenged is never a pleasant process. But it is something we must do if we want to "shape the future in accordance with high ideals." Are we willing to ask questions that may render our current understanding of the world inadequate? What if these questions challenge those ideas we hold most dear? In the end, we have a choice. Do we want to live in reality and weigh what we believe against all the facts? Or do we want to live in a world that does not exist because it is easier to believe a fantasy?

The ideas put forth in this book will raise a lot of questions without immediate answers. But we have a moral obligation to walk this path. At times the way may seem unclear, and we may want to turn back to old and familiar—though faulty—ideas. But if we want to understand the destiny of this great nation, we must press on. I hope you will join me in this journey, and together we can see the rebirth of a nation.

Sean Edwards
Spokane, WA

ᛒ AMERICAN
RESURRECTION ᘓ

Chapter 1

HOW THE CONSTITUTION FAILED... AND NOBODY NOTICED

"Remember, democracy never lasts long. It soon wastes, exhausts, and murders itself. There never was a democracy yet that did not commit suicide."

~ John Adams ~

The U.S. Constitution has failed. Its failure is so expansive and extensive we cannot fix it with a mere corrective law or Amendment. But most don't even realize that it has failed, and that is far more troublesome in itself.

The government has violated the intent of the Constitution so much that it has become the very thing the founders sought to abolish. As an example, since 2011, Congress has passed a version of the National Defense Authorization Act (NDAA) that includes a provision that gives the President power to hold American citizens for an indefinite amount of time.

To do this, the government only needs to believe that the individual may be a terrorist. They do not need evidence to make the arrest. They do not have to file charges. They do not have to tell the person why they have been arrested. The individual is not guaranteed a trial. Nor are they allowed access to legal council. This provision overturns every right guaranteed by the 4th and 6th Amendments of the Constitution.

The 4th Amendment guarantees that the government must obtain a warrant to search or seize a person or their property. And to get a warrant, they must take an oath or provide an affidavit to a judge as to the just cause of the search or seizure.

The 6th Amendment guarantees that in any criminal prosecution, the defendant gets a fair and speedy trial (not held indefinitely) by a jury of their peers. It also states that the defendant must be informed of the nature and cause of their prosecution. Finally, they are also guaranteed the right to legal council.

The Indefinite Detention clause of the NDAA violates all of these provisions.

The fact that this law even exists should catalyze

the American people into action. But it hasn't, and that is far more dangerous.

Though the NDAA is a glaring example of our Constitution's failure, it is not alone. The lives of individuals are violated by the government on a daily basis. Things like drug-use prohibitions, anti-prostitution laws, gay marriage bans, and even welfare programs all violate a person's freedom. These things point to a systemic failure in our Constitution.

These points may not seem like failures to some, but that is why this book is necessary. We don't realize that many of our government programs violate the Constitution on a daily basis.

Part of this failure comes from the fact that we no longer understand the purpose of government. We should be asking questions like: Why does government exist? What is it supposed to do? Where does it get its power? And what are its limits?

Very few people ask these kinds of questions today, because most assume they already know the answers. But when asked to crystalize their understanding of government into one sentence, most people can not.

We have become so disconnected with why our Constitution exists that we can't even see that it has become powerless to accomplish what it was meant to do. If Americans understood the purpose behind their Constitution, its failure would be obvious.

Misperceptions of Government

Today, many believe that government should protect Judeo-Christian values. They may not want to make Christianity the national religion, but they do want key aspects of the Christian moral code to form our laws. Thereby "protecting" society and establishing a "righteous government."

Though born of good intentions, this construct has led to some horrible atrocities in history. The Spanish Inquisition and the Crusades are just two examples.

If Judeo-Christian values are to form the basis of a righteous government, then who decides what becomes law? Which aspects of the Christian faith should we fashion into legislation? Should we outlaw adultery? Or lying? Or having a faith other than our own? Where do we draw the line?

How, then, are we any different than those countries that stone people for committing adultery? Their laws are based on their faith, and they choose to impose their beliefs on those around them – just as we do. This presents some serious issues for a free society. What happens when other people with a different moral code than ours get into office? What happens if they pass laws – based on their faith – that puts us into chains?

Many Americans think our representative government gives us the *carte blanche* right to determine what is legal. The argument goes, "We have a representative government, so I have the freedom to decide what laws I want and what laws I don't." Though this makes sense at first, it soon breaks down. It means that the majority defines morality. With this line of thinking, as long as the majority agrees, anything can be written into law. There are no safeguards, and this sets up the tyranny of the majority.

At one point, we decided to round up all Japanese-Americans and put them in internment camps. We also decided that the "separate but equal" laws of the south were acceptable. We decided that women couldn't vote. And we determined that Native Americans did not deserve the protection of their civil rights.

This view of government fails to protect people from the whims of the masses. People, even in majority, are fallible. They can and do make mistakes. How, then, can we with good conscience force people to live by what the majority believes is right? What if the majority decided that stealing is legal? Or murder? Or rape?

If we think in these terms, then where do we draw the line? How do we protect ourselves from the dictatorship of the masses? We cannot maintain freedom when the majority can determine what is right and wrong.

What happens when a new majority gains power with a different set of values than our own? We have already set the precedent that anything can become law. Now, there is nothing protecting us from their edicts. Our freedom could disappear over night.

We need something more concrete to protect us.

That is what the founding fathers were trying to establish. And that is the original purpose behind the Constitution.

The Constitution is an imperfect enumeration of a more perfect idea. This idea transcends any particular faith or man-made moral code. It is steadfast and solid throughout time. It is unchanging and unyielding. It

---

The Constitution is an imperfect enumeration of a more perfect idea.

---

alone has the power to establish and protect our freedom. And it alone as the ability to create a moral government.

When crafting the Constitution, the founders knew they were establishing a raw government. They charged later generations to refine the Constitution as they found its weaknesses. Yet those weaknesses have proven too great over the years. We need a much more dramatic solution than a simple amendment.

Today, we have forgotten the radical ideas laid out by our founding fathers. The crafters assumed Americans would stay educated in the principles of freedom. Yet, we have not, and the original design of our country has become murky. Instead of anchoring our purpose and charting our course, the Constitution has become a lighthouse lost at sea. It is tossed and turned by the waves of an ever-changing political climate.

With that said, the ideas behind the Constitution have not failed. They are so timeless and powerful that they can never die. Even if they burn out for a time, they will rise again. That is what this book will attempt to do.

The Current Disaster

Our errors have caused our entire political system to go off course. No party holds the corner on a righteous government. The water has become cloudy. Truth and fallacy, right and wrong have become skewed. We are no longer the shining light to the world. Our lamp has gone dark. We may have the most powerful military, but we no longer hold the moral and philosophical high ground. We are devouring ourselves in a confused struggle to do what is right.

The American political system has failed to accomplish its primary mission: to protect the individual at all costs. As we will illustrate in the coming chapters, protecting the individual is the sole reason why our country exists. And this should be the one and only agenda of public policy. This is not because we have an inflated view of the individual. But rather because we understand the commanding nature of equality. There is no middle ground. There is no grey area. It is either equality or tyranny. The choice belongs to us.

This book is a plea to remind us of our great purpose. It is an attempt to reignite the fire that turned the world upside down. It is a battle cry to reawaken the sleeping giant to do it again.

What lies before us is a choice that will affect generations to come. This choice is between right and wrong, and black and white. We have the chance to remember who we are. We have the chance to transform the world around us. We have the chance to change the course of human history, just as our forefathers did before us. We have the chance to see the rebirth of a nation. This is the American Resurrection.

Chapter 2

THE FORGOTTEN REASONS
WHY AMERICA EXISTS

"I entirely concur in the propriety of resorting to
the sense in which the Constitution was accepted
and ratified by the nation. *In that sense alone it is
the legitimate Constitution.*"

~ *James Madison* ~

The central idea that led to America's creation was
based on the belief that every human being was created equal to one another. We have repeated this
phrase so often in modern times that we no longer
understand its meaning. Once we understand the
full power of equality, it will challenge some of the
cornerstones of modern government.

True equality means that each person has complete sovereignty over their own life, and no power on earth can violate it. The argument comes from the idea that creation grants authority and ownership.

If you cut down a tree and craft a table from it, the table belongs to you. The table did not create itself. You made it. And unless you give it away, no one has the right to it–because it is yours.

In the same way, no one is self-made, nor is anyone made by another. Just like the table, God is the sole author of life, and thus the sole authority over life.[2] God is the only person who "owns" us. He alone created us; He alone has the right to destroy us; and He alone has the right to dictate our lives.

This means that in relation to each other, person-to-person, we are completely equal to one another. We have no authority over another. We cannot end

---

2. Some might think that parenthood give parents a certain right over their children. One cannot confuse the act of procreation with creating life itself. There is a big difference between having sex and designing a human being. We do not grant another person consciousness or the ability to think. Our part in the process is minimal, while nature does the rest.

Parenthood does not give us ownership over another. Instead we are stewarding an individual to become a self-functioning adult. Children are not capable of making appropriate decisions in life. Thus the role of the parent is to make decisions for the child until the child has fully developed into a person. But there comes a time when those children mature and step into their sovereignty as individuals.

the lives of others. We cannot steal from others. We cannot dictate the lives of others. Doing so would be a violation of God's ownership and lordship.

It doesn't matter if people accept God as their creator or not, He still created them, and thus He still

---

Inherent equality goes beyond all theology and religion.

---

owns them. We cannot claim one ounce of ownership over their lives. People's equality simply exists by the very nature of mankind. It is inherent to our beings, and cannot be morally divorced from our person by any power on earth.

This "inherent" equality goes beyond any theology or religion. It transcends all man made codes of morality, institutions, or beliefs by simply existing.

You do not need to believe in God to arrive at the same conclusion. You only need reason. Nature produces all life. Thus, the children of nature have certain rights in relation to each other.

As an illustration, take pine trees. One pine tree is not more of a pine tree than another. One may be bigger or older, but on a cellular level, they are both pine trees. One does not hold a higher "title" of pine tree. They are utterly equal. In the same way, people are entirely equal. We may be bigger or smaller, lighter or darker, but no one is more "homo sapien" than another.

Whether you believe in God, or that humanity is a product of nature, it doesn't change the fact that everyone has an equal claim to "homo sapien." No one is more human than their neighbor. Their existence, and their equality to each other, is granted to them by the very fact that they exist.

In this way every person is equal to one another. This equality affords individual basic rights that no power on earth can breach. Those rights include: 1) The right to life, 2) The right to determine how you live your life (freedom), and 3) And the right to the products of your life's labor.

The right to life should be obvious at this point. No one has the right to end or harm your life. Any transgression of this right is murder.

The right to freedom should also be clear. No one has the right to dictate your life. Any transgression of this right is slavery.

The right to your personal wealth may seem less obvious. But consider your labor as an extension of your life. Since you exhausted time and energy from your life in that labor, the fruits of your labor only exist because of your life. Thus, they are an extension of your life. This means that no one has a right to them but you. Any transgression of this right is theft.

No power on earth can morally tip this equality. No person can ethically violate it. No State can justly overturn it. God (or Nature) are the only entities that have the right to do those things.

The Only Way To Tip Equality

There is one way we can tip equality: self-defense. When someone tries to harm us, they have disobeyed the natural equality of all people and made themselves lord over us. They have declared a superior title of "homo sapien" and claimed a right to our lives. They have decided to act like a wild animal that takes what it pleases. They have made themselves a danger to society.

If people violate our inherent equality, we have the right to defend ourselves and reclaim what they stole from us. This is the only way in which a person can take power over another in a moral manner. In its purest form, this is justice. Justice seeks to protect and restore the inherent rights of all people.

In a perfect world, people would be responsible for their own justice. This would make government unnecessary. But this also would never work in actual society. People are too tempted to embellish the truth in the heat of the moment. False accusations and exaggerations would run rampant. Chaos would ensue (think of the Red Scare or the Salem Witch Trials).

This poses a problem for us. How do we recognize the equality of all people and at the same time bring order to the streets? How do we protect the inherent rights of individuals while preserving justice?

This is the point at which we discover the only acceptable foundation of governmental power. This is the question that will lead us to what a righteous government looks like. And the answer to this question will reveal what our Constitution was attempting to implement.

To preserve justice and respect the inherent rights of all individuals, people must voluntarily lay down their right to seek their own justice and empower an objective third party to administer justice. A group of people must come together and empower an impartial third party to enforce the inherent equality of all. In short, the unbiased Rule of Law must protect the rights of the individual from every other party. This is the sole moral responsibility of government. Otherwise, the government itself will violate the rights of the individual, something that it has no ethical power to do.

In other words, government literally gains its power from the people. It exists because they have offered up a part of their authority for the sake of Justice. It cannot exist apart from that consent.

This means that government cannot have any more power than individuals. If its existence stems from the natural rights of individuals, how could it have more power than the total of its parts? If you, as an individual, do not have the ethical right to do something, then neither does the government.

This also means that the government gains a legal monopoly over violence. It is the only entity that can

---

The unbiased rule of law must protect the rights of the individual ... this is the sole moral responsibility of government.

---

use the threat of force to motivate people into action. Which is a good thing, as long as the people keep that monopoly in check.

Without the ability to use force, the government would be powerless to protect its people. That power is a deterrent against would-be thieves or assailants. Without it, people would live under constant fear that their fellow man could at any moment assault them. Without the protection government offers, people cannot be free to live their own lives. They would live at the mercy of their neighbors.

In short, the inherent rights of humanity cannot be

made a reality without government. Government is the instrument that makes equality tangible in people's lives. Freedom may be an inherent right granted to all by nature. But as long as there are murders and thieves in the world, freedom isn't a reality until we empower a government to implement it.

The Heart of the Constitution

This is the idea that gave birth to our Constitution. The Constitution was intended to establish a government that held the equality of all people as its highest ideal. It would make the protection of the individual its supreme responsibility. Every law should be bound by the truth that no man has the right to dictate the life of another.

Yet, other individuals are not the only entities that can violate our natural rights. As was just stated, the government has an exclusive use of force against individuals. We need this monopoly on violence for the sake of harmony in the streets, but we must also restrain it for obvious reasons.

The founders knew the government would become the aggressor if it wasn't limited to protecting the individual. They knew that without restrictions, the majority could easily oppress minorities and individuals.

Thus, the Constitution also sought to establish a

binding framework that kept the government from violating the rights of the individual.

The Constitution was our way of granting the government the powers necessary to make freedom a reality, while at the same time limiting those powers. It spells out the rights we have given the government for the sake of establishing freedom. The Constitution itself is an attempt to make this idea of individual equality a reality. It also limited how the government could use its power in order to protect the individual from the government itself.

This means that we must interpret the Constitution through this lens. Otherwise it will be (and has been) used to do things contrary to the reason it exists.

The founders understood that they were trying to do something that had never been done before. They knew they wouldn't get it perfect the first time. That is why they left room for future generations to refine the Constitution (through the amendment process). They knew it was imperfect, and we need to as well. Yet, they assumed (or prayed) that we would do this within the context of individual equality. But we have not.

The idea of equality is so radical, and so powerful that it still challenges us today. When we understand it, we can see just how far our government has drifted from the intent of the Constitution. The Constitution has been used time and time again to violate the lives of individuals. Politicians have used the Constitution as proof that the government has the right to override certain individual rights. They have used the Constitution to support slavery, civil liberties violations, internment camps, oppressive religion based morality, and even welfare programs. All of which require some violation of individual rights.

This is how our Constitution has failed. Over the course of two hundred and fifty years, it has not protected our inherent rights. Little by little, we have lost touch with what our founders were trying to do. We have allowed our government to become the thing from which the Constitution was supposed to protect us.

In the following chapters we will look at this in more depth and show how the Constitution has failed to protect the equality of all.

Chapter 3

THE RISE OF RELIGIOUS TYRANNY IN THE U.S.

"Power always thinks... that it is doing God's service when it is violating all his laws."

∽ John Adams ∽

Contrary to popular opinion, the United States is not a Christian nation, nor was it ever meant to be. The crafters of the Constitution wanted to set up our government to be separate from religion.

Their attempt to separate the church from the state is evident by the First Amendment: "Congress shall make no law respecting an establishment of religion, or prohibiting the free exercise thereof."

We have become so disconnected with the concept

of equality that many Christians don't even believe in the separation of church and state. You often hear Christians say, "you can't find 'the separation of church and state' in the Constitution." Implying that the Constitution allows for the morality of our Christian faith to influence law. The phrase "the separation of church and state" may never appear in the Constitution. But that does not mean that the founders intended for the moral precepts of our faith to guide lawmaking. This confusion reveals just how far we have drifted from the idea of inherent equality.

The crafters didn't use this exact phrase because they would have thought it absurd to think otherwise. It would be like reading the New Testament and saying, "the scriptures never actually say that God exists." It is a presupposition that you cannot divorce from the content of scripture. In the same way, you cannot divorce the separation of church and state from the intent of our Constitution.

The concepts of equality permeated the founders' political and philosophical world. The idea that the Constitution could allow religious morality to guide lawmaking would have seemed impossible to them. They knew that forcing the religious precepts of any faith on another would violate their freedom. You can easily force people to live by the precepts of the Christian faith without saying, "you have to be

Christian to live here." Just outlaw gay marriage. Or tell them they can't drink alcohol. Or smoke marijuana. Or outlaw prostitution.

Prostitution is illegal in almost every corner of America. We have outlawed the use of marijuana, cocaine, and heroine. 32 States have banned gay marriage. And 19 of them have constitutional amendments keeping gay marriage from ever becoming legal.

The existence of these laws proves that the Constitution has failed.

None of these actions impact anyone other than the people consenting to take part in them. There is no theft, murder, assault, or rape. No one is forcing himself or herself onto another.

In the case of prostitution, there are two consenting adults choosing to partake in a sex-for-money trade. With gay marriage, two consenting adults are choosing to live together and call it marriage. Who, in these equations, are having their rights violated?

These activities are illegal because we believe our Christian faith says they are wrong. In essence, the majority has decided to force their morality onto those around them.

As long as someone's choices do not violate the rights of another, the government cannot concern itself with it. Otherwise, we, through the government, have violated the law of equality. We have taken God's place of lordship over others by telling them how to live their lives. When has God given us the right to do that? When did nature determine who could order the lives of others?

If we outlaw these activities because we think they are wrong, where do we draw the line? What stops us from banning adultery, divorce, drunkenness, or lying? None of these actions on their own violate an individual's personal freedom, but we think they are wrong.

By enacting these kinds of laws, we are establishing a theocracy no different than those around the world that execute people for adultery. We are not recognizing people's God-given freedom to live their own lives. We are forcing our morality onto them. And we are putting them into chains.

When we allow our religious morality to dictate the laws of a country, any law could be passed as long as it can get enough supporters. There are no safeguards. There are no limits.

The First Amendment was meant to be this safeguard. It was supposed to protect us from these kinds of laws, but it has failed.

Our nation was not unique because it was Christian. It was not unique because it was based on Christian ideals. It wasn't even unique because it was a democracy.

All other Western nations at that time were Christian and worked from a Christian worldview. And many of them had blended democracy into their governments. These ideas were not new.

Our nation was unique because it was based on the idea that all people were created equal. It was special because it established that no man had authority over another. It was exceptional because it recognized that no power on earth could morally violate that freedom. This was a revolutionary idea. It paved the way for the first moral government to have ever existed. One that recognized the holiness of every person's life and dared not violate a person's freedom. Ayn Rand wrote, "The United States of America is the greatest, the noblest and, in its original founding principles, the only moral country in the history of the world."[3]

Laws based on religious morality reveal how our Constitution has failed to protect a person's freedom. We should never have debated issues such as same-sex marriage and drug-use in the political arena. They do not belong in the realm of politics. If we continue to push for these kinds of laws, we are fighting to destroy our moral government. Not only that, but we are advancing religious tyranny. We may not like how others live their lives, but we have no right to tell

---

3. Ayn Rand, *Philosophy: Who Needs It?*

them how to do so. Otherwise, we are no different than tyrants.[4]

Laws Do Not Endorse Activities

There is a fear that if we lifted these laws, we would be "condoning" the actions they prohibit, and that acceptance would weaken our country. But this would not happen.

Laws are not a statement on what we think is right and wrong. Laws should have one purpose: To ensure that you may live your life how ever you see fit, free from the threat of others. Beyond that, laws have no right to exist.

They are not a moral treatise on our culture, nor a list of unacceptable activities. Thus, lifting these laws would not be an acceptance of those activities.

There is also a fear that if we allow people to do as they wish, it would weaken the moral foundation of our country. There is a fear that the culture would decay and our nation would collapse.

Yet, our laws are not effectively prohibiting these actions now. People are still buying drugs. Sex-for-money transactions still occur. In fact, instead of

---

4. For more information on why Christians should support legalizing gay marriage, see *Gay Marriage: Why Conservative Christians Need To Support It.*

prohibiting these activities, they actually make them more dangerous by pushing them into the criminal world. If someone wants drugs, they have to partner with murders, rapists, and thugs to get them. In essence, our laws fund the criminal underworld.

If we lifted these laws, our society would not collapse. We would just see it for what it really is. And, billions of dollars would no longer fund drug cartels, pimps, thugs, and thieves.

The Law As A Cultural Steward

Some feel that the law should be a "steward" to help people stay out of harmful activities when they don't know better. But the government is not a parent. As long as their choices do not harm others, we do not have the right to tell them how to live their lives. even if that lifestyle contradicts our sense of morality. People are people, and they get to choose their own lives. We do not get to choose it for them. That is called slavery.

Will there be more experimentation in these activities? Maybe. But will our society spiral out of control? No. There is little evidence to support that conclusion. Especially sense many of these activities weren't criminalized until the 20th century.[5] Since they didn't destroy our nation then, why would they now?

Many also see the laws of a nation as a litmus test for the morality of that nation. According to this view, legalizing something is the same as saying, "we as a society–to some degree–believe this action is good and proper."

As we have already discussed, laws of a nation should never make these kinds of judgments. They should be limited to the protection of the individual. Thus, just because something is legal doesn't mean it is moral. It just means that we recognize people have the right to choose how to live their own lives.

---

5. As an example, the Harrison Act of 1914 is the first recorded federal ban on the distribution of drugs in the United States. http://www. princeton.edu/~achaney/tmve/wiki100k/docs/Harrison_Narcotics_ Tax_Act.html Accessed on February 6th, 2014.

Chapter 4

WHY SOCIETY SHOULD NOT BE GOVERNED

"Individual rights are not subject to a public vote;
a majority has no right to vote away the rights
of a minority; the political function of rights is
precisely to protect minorities from oppression
by majorities – *and the smallest minority on earth
is the individual.*"

∼ *Ayn Rand* ∼

To understand freedom, the first thing we need to
realize is that government and society are not the
same things. Yet, this is exactly what many people
believe (if even only subconsciously).

This shift in thought has led to some significant

confusion about the role of government. During most policy debates you can hear arguments about what "society" should and shouldn't do. But society and government are not the same things, and to treat them as such is a mistake. The *Merriam-Webster Dictionary* defines "society" as such:

> "a : an enduring and cooperating social group whose members have developed organized patterns of relationships through interaction with one another
>
> b : a community, nation, or broad grouping of people having common traditions, institutions, and collective activities and interests"

Society is a community of individuals that have developed a common way of interacting with each other.

For instance, the institution of shaking hands when first meeting someone is part of our society. Celebrating birthdays is an institution that is part of our society.

Having a 9-5 job is an expectation that is a part of our society. Society, in this sense, is large and expansive. Government is just one part of society that harmonizes the interactions between individuals. Government is not society itself.

Some people may think this is a semantic argument, yet it is not. Because we have blurred the lines between society and government with our words, our deeds are following suit. What we once deemed a "societal" issue is now described as a "political" one, and vice versa. Today, we see public welfare, job creation, and economic development as the responsibility of the government. But there was a time when we would have said that these were private sector issues, and that the government did not have the right to intervene in them.

Can you imagine what the world would look like if we followed this association to its end? All cultural issues, traditions, and collective interests would receive government oversight and legislation. When we equate government and society with our words, we are setting a course for our actions that can lead us down a road we do not want to travel.

Society is nothing more than a collection of individuals, and we cannot treat it as anything else. As an example, a vehicle is made of metal, rubber, and plastic. But it can do things that metal, rubber, and plastic cannot on their own. In this sense, it can do more than the sum of its parts, just as society is more complex than the sum of its parts (the individual).

But a car is still governed by the same laws that dictate metal, rubber, and plastic. Just because a car can transport you over long distances doesn't mean its parts can't wear down. You must maintain your vehicle and treat it for what it is.

In the same sense, individuals make up society, and we must treat it as such. We must have rules for society, but those rules cannot violate the fundamental building blocks of society: the individual.

This means that you cannot have laws that violate the rights of the individual for the "good of society." When we do this, we are saying that some people have the right to dictate the lives of others.

We are saying that the needs of some warrant violating the equality of others.

We are saying that the majority has the right to control the minority.

Who gave us this authority? When did we gain the right to do this?

This is wrong, and we should never allow it.

Chapter 5

YOUR WEALTH IS YOUR LIFE

"We hold these truths to be self-evident, that all men are created equal, that they are endowed by their Creator with certain unalienable Rights, that among these are Life, Liberty and *the Pursuit of Happiness.*"

~ *Thomas Jefferson* ~

Thomas Jefferson immortalized the political rationale for the American Revolution in the above quote. We've already looked at Life and Liberty, but what did the founders mean when they said people had an unalienable right to the pursuit of happiness?

If we look at the context of the Revolution, we can see that the founders were referring to the right to own property (or possess wealth).

The Declaration appears to be referencing John Locke's *Second Treatise on Government*. Locke said that every person was born with the right to "life, liberty, and property."[6] Thomas Jefferson changed "property" to the "pursuit of happiness." This implies that the founders linked owning property with pursuing happiness.

The Virginia Declaration of Rights supports this argument. It equates "pursuing happiness" with possessing property:

> "That all men are by nature equally free and independent, and have certain inherent rights, of which, when they enter into a state of society, they cannot, by any compact, deprive or divest their posterity; namely, the enjoyment of life and liberty, with the means of *acquiring and possessing property*, and pursuing and obtaining happiness and safety."[7]

In the 18th century, the word "property" meant something different than it does today. It referred to something over which you had control. For instance, someone from the 18th century may have said, "I have property in my house." Meaning that he, and he alone, had authority over his house.

---

6. John Locke, *Two Treatises of Government*, Cambridge: Cambridge University Press. sec 87, 123, 209, 222

7. Virginia Declaration of Rights, Adopted in 1776

Thus, people have a property in their own lives and all that they own. Land and wealth fall under this definition.

The founders believed that your possessions were an extension of your life. This meant that you, and you alone, had a right to them.

To illustrate this, let's look at an apple tree. If an apple tree grows in the wild, its apples belong to everyone. Anyone can pick an apple from it without it being theft.

Yet, if you pick an apple, and someone takes that apple from you as you walk down the street, we would consider it theft. Why? What happened that made that apple yours? How did it go from belonging to everyone to belonging to you?

Quite simply... *you picked it.*

Your labor to retrieve it made it yours. If it were not for you and your labor, that apple would still be on the tree. This means that the apple is yours, and no one has a right to take it from you.

Now let's look at a bigger picture. If you take an empty field, plow it, plant apple seeds, and grow an orchard, to whom do those apples belong? They belong to you and no one else. Even though anyone can pick the apples on a tree in the wild, they cannot pick apples from your trees. Why? Because those trees exist by your labor. Your time, labor, and energy went into making empty land produce fruit. Thus, that fruit belongs to you and no one else.

As we will see, the Constitution was designed to protect the fruit of your labor. That is what it means to be free, and that is what our founders envisioned. Unfortunately, in modern times we have muddied these waters.

Chapter 6

MONEY: THE ROOT
OF ALL GOOD

"All wealth is the product of labor."

~ George Poulett Scrope ~

The term "money" can mean many different things to different people. There is a vague, undefined understanding of money that can lead to apathy towards fiscal policy. Some have even gone so far as to despise money. They see it as responsible for economic inequality in the world.

Yet, money is vitally important to society. And it is imperative that the government honor your money as yours. The government cannot take your money for any other reason than to protect you. Otherwise, it has violated your life and stolen from you.

Your Money Is An Extension Of Your Person

As we have already discussed, labor is an extension of your life. And money is the product of your labor converted into something that anyone can use. Your money is your labor. This means that we should not despise it. We should celebrate it.

Despite many misconceptions about money, it is brilliant. It allows us to trade our skills and services to anyone, even if they don't need our specific skill or service. An example will help illustrate this.

Let's say the owner of an apple orchard went to a plumber for his services. As long has the plumber needed some apples, they could do an even trade. But if the plumber didn't need apples, but rather milk, then the orchard owner would have to find a farmer who needed apples. He would then have to trade his apples for milk so that he could then trade that milk for plumbing services.

As you can see, this simple trade system (also known as a "barter system") can become very complicated very quickly.

Fortunately, people simplified the process long ago with a money system. They began trading their products or services for an item everyone valued. Since everyone valued this one item, they could then trade it for anything they wanted. It became a "trade medium."

This way they didn't have to worry about the complexities of a simple barter system.

If everyone valued one item, lets say salt for example (which many ancient societies did), you could trade your apples for salt. Then you could trade that salt for anything else you needed, like plumbing services (because he could then trade it for anything he needed).

We have records showing that different societies used different items throughout history for this purpose. Some cultures used odd items like salt or butter. But gold and silver took the top two preferred seats.

In modern times we traded precious metals for currency notes. This is what we have today. At first, a $1 bill represented ½₀^th of an ounce of gold in the bank. This meant that you could take that note to a bank and get ½₀^th of an ounce of gold whenever you wished.

All this to say that money is nothing more than your labor converted into something that everyone values.

Not everyone wants apples, but money allows you to convert those apples into something that everyone does want. Then you can use that money for anything you might need.

The money system is brilliant. It streamlines transactions and makes everyone's labor available to everyone else.

What does this mean, and why is it important to us? *At the end of the day, your money is your labor.* It is what you produce. You may have sold your apples and only have dollars in your pocket, but those dollars represent your labor, and is thus an extension of your life.

Value Is Subjective

Furthermore, what we use as money does not determine money's value. Some believe that we need to return to a gold standard because gold has inherent value, while paper doesn't.

It is easy to think that gold is valuable because it is gold (presumably because it is rare). Yet, there is no inherent value in gold. It is just a metal that we pull from the ground. There are plenty of other things that are rare that we do not consider valuable. The reason we as a society value gold is because we value it. That's it.

There is even less inherent value in a dollar bill. With gold, you could at least argue that there is some sort of inherent value because we can use it as a commodity itself (in jewelry or electronics). But a dollar bill is just paper. We can't use dollar bills for anything other than money. Yet we, as a society, have decided that it has value. We decided that it represents our labor and productive capacity. That's the only reason it is valuable. It doesn't matter if it is gold, silver, green pieces of paper, or butter, as long as society agrees that it represents our labor, then it can work as money.

Also, the "purchasing power" of money (the quantity of something money can buy) is not set in stone. It is subjective.

If you have a barrel of apples, you have a price in your mind of what they are worth. You have determined that a certain amount of money is a good trade for your time and labor. Someone who wants to buy those apples has to make a similar assessment. What are those apples worth to them? How much of their time and labor (converted into dollars) is worth a barrel of your apples? If your price is too high, the two of you may negotiate, or that person may buy apples from someone else.

Thus, the "purchasing power" of money is entirely subjective. Both parties in a transaction determine it. There is no "inherent" value in the apples or the money. The two people making the trade determine the value of both.

This is important because it reveals one crucial fact about life: money doesn't exist! Money, or the value that money has, is only determined by our agreement. This means that it only exists in our minds. If the value of something is only determined by our agreement, then how can it exist in a tangible way in the world? It can't, and it doesn't.

This means that money is immaterial and that there is no limit to the wealth in the world. It doesn't matter that there is a limited number of dollars in the world, because a dollar's value is determined by our agreement. Nothing more.

Have you heard the saying, "For some to be rich, others have to be poor?" This phrase comes from the idea that there is only so much money in the world. It implies that if you want more money, you have to take it from someone else. But if wealth is infinite, then this argument falls apart.

There is not a finite amount of wealth in the world. We can create wealth out of nothing. A new idea, innovation, or product can increase the wealth in the world. Wealth is unlimited. The only thing limiting wealth is how we think about money.

Capitalism: A Modern Marvel

If wealth is unlimited, and money is the representation of our labor, then we cannot consider money evil. If we do so, we are calling man's productive capacity evil. And we are saying that man's ability to produce – and trade between each other – is evil.

There are only two ways that goods and services can pass between people: by trade or by force. People can either willingly trade their goods and services with each other in a way that benefits both parties. Or one must take those goods and services by force. There is no other option.

There are many people who claim that capitalism is evil, or that we should at least restrain it. But, the act of trading with each other is capitalism. If we declare capitalism to be evil, the only other option left is theft. If we call capitalism evil, it implies that theft is good.

If wealth is unlimited, and money is the representation of our labor, then we cannot consider money evil.

We may not like how people trade their money, but it is their money. It is a product of their life. We have no right to it. We cannot tell them how to use it, or take it from them by force.

Furthermore, capitalism allows people to work with each other in a way that benefits both parties. Walter E. Williams put it this way:

> "Prior to capitalism, the way people amassed great wealth was by looting, plundering, and enslaving their fellow man. Capitalism made it possible to become wealthy by serving your fellow man."

The ability to freely trade between people has produced more wealth in the last two hundred years than the world has ever seen. Even the poorest of the poor are wealthier than they have ever been in human history.

Money represents how other people value what you do. When people trade, they serve each other and work in harmony. In this way, we have made it possible to become wealthy by serving our fellow man.

We should not despise money and the capitalistic system of free trade. They drive us forward. They push us into new realms of innovation and possibility. They represent man's ability to create something out of nothing.

We should celebrate the development of capitalism in the western world as a modern marvel. It transformed humanity from a poor, barbaric society into a prosperous, civilized people. It represents our maturity from raiding thugs into enlightened equals. It illustrates our transition from stealing to creating. Capitalism is proof that humanity can better itself.

Chapter 7

SLAVERY 2.0: A BOOMING AMERICAN BUSINESS

"We are ready to accept almost any explanation of the present crisis of our civilization except one: that the present state of the world may be the result of genuine error on our own part."

∼ Friedrich Hayek ∼

Many people believe that there is a moral demand on society to take care of the least among us. This often takes the form of a government-run assistance program (or "welfare"). Yet, the nature of money and the role of government make government-run welfare immoral.

Assisting the poor should be a high priority for

society. But government should never be the instrument of social change. When we use government to enact social change, it only has one tool that it can use: Cooperation by threat of violence.

The government must get the money it needs for assistance programs somewhere. It cannot just create the money it needs.[8] It must first collect taxes. When we impose a tax to pay for welfare, we are forcing individuals to support a social program with which they may or may not agree.

We have become desensitized to the moral problems this raises. When the IRS demands your money, you must pay. If you don't, they can seize your property and throw you in jail (compliance by the threat of force). The government should have the ability to force people to pay their taxes. But that power should only be used to protect individuals, not force them to fund a charity program.

---

8. This is not entirely true. Governments can print more money, but this is not "creating money." In reality, it is a hidden tax that allows a government to pay for things without asking its people for more taxes.

Often governments need to pay for the things but don't want to raise taxes. Usually they are wars or promised social programs. Without taxing people, they are left with two options: borrow money, or print more money. Printing is the easier of the two options, but it is one of the most anti-democratic things a government can do. [continued on next page]

If someone came into your house, pulled a gun, and demanded that you pay them $5,000, you would call it theft. It wouldn't matter if they told you they would use it for a good purpose. They would be taking money from you without your consent. Theft is theft.

But when the IRS does it, it doesn't seem wrong. We may not like it, but we don't see it as a crime. Just because something has been legislated doesn't mean it is right.

A welfare system demands (it does not ask) that some people work to support others. We are saying that some have the right to force others to support

---

When a burst of new money floods a market, the market is slow to adjust. Over time, this will cause the purchasing power of each dollar to devalue. This means that you need more dollars to buy the same amount of goods. But it takes time for the market to adjust, so we don't notice it right away. During this time, the government gets to spend their newly printed money at its current (higher) value. But as the price of goods and services begin to adjust, individual paychecks stay the same. Some people enjoy a regular "cost of living" raise, but the raise is not immediate. During this interim time, your paycheck isn't able to purchase what it used to. I.e., you have less money.

In essence, the government has taken a part of your paycheck in a deceptive, indirect manner. They did not tax you. If they had, you could see upfront how much of your labor went into to funding their program. By printing the money they needed, they basically made your paycheck smaller (in what it can purchase).

Even more troubling, the Federal Government doesn't need congressional approval to do this. This is taxation without representation. It is quite possibly one of the most anti-democratic things a government can do, and it should stop immediately.

them with their labor. This is nothing more than a watered down version of slavery.

The Needs of the Many...

You may have heard it said, "The needs of the many out weigh the needs of the few." This sentiment is used to justify taking money from some (the few) in order to help those in need (the many).

What people are really saying is, "The needs of the many outweigh the *rights* of the few." Meaning, the needs of some justify the violation of some people's rights.

Yet, this means that we have built a society where minorities, or individuals (the smallest minority) are sacrificed for the sake of the majority. One person's need cannot justify the violation of another person's rights.

If we look back at the apple orchard example, when does someone's need guarantee them the right to take your apples? How much of your labor belongs to them? And why?

We do not have a greater duty to society than to individuals. Society is just a collection of individuals. How can one individual have a right to another's life? Welfare says that one person's needs justify robbing someone else. This is never right.

Do The Ends Justify The Means?

Some people may believe that in order to accomplish good, the ends may justify the means. But in any partnership between good and evil, it is only evil that can profit.

No matter how noble our intent, we cannot justify taking someone's wealth by force, even for the advancement of another. It is nothing more than legislated

---

One person's need cannot justify the violation of another person's rights.

---

theft and slavery. Those who advocate welfare are pursuing a noble cause. But the ends cannot justify the means. We cannot steal from one and give to another. No power on earth gives us that right. By writing welfare into law, we are allowing ideological tyranny to exist in our country.

If we decide that some individuals get to dictate how others live their lives, then we are living in a brutal society that is experiencing a momentary period of peace.

If we allow the majority to decide our morality, then at any moment our laws could change to suit a new majority. We may like the idea of giving the government power to help the poor. But once the government has that power, someone else can come along and use it for an entirely different purpose.

To use our apple orchard example again, once the majority has this power, they could decide that your apple orchard now belongs to them. All of your time and labor could be seized in a heartbeat. Then, they could force you to continue to work it "for the greater good" (by making it illegal to change occupations). Does this seem absurd? It has happened again and again in modern history. Democratically elected governments have fallen into this kind of bondage by stepping closer and closer to socialism via expanding welfare programs.

We may like the *idea* that the needs of the many outweigh the rights of the few, but that philosophy opens the door to dangerous possibilities. There is truth in the old adage that the road to hell is paved with good intentions.

A government's sole purpose is to protect the individual. If we don't protect the equality of all people, we too may someday find ourselves in chains to the majority.

If the government itself robs the individual, then it has become the thing our founding fathers set out to stop. Any area where our government does not protect the individual, it has no moral grounds to exist. Otherwise it will become the thief and the brute.

In reality, there is no conflict between society and the individual. To suggest otherwise implies that the equality of some should be sacrificed to the interests of others. This is not just. One person does not have the right to lay claim to another's life.

Charity is good. However, government enforced "charity" is wrong. To quote Terry Goodkind, "Charity has to be completely voluntary. Or else it just becomes a nice word for slavery."

Walter E. Williams echoed the sentiment when he said:

> "What's 'just' has been debated for centuries but let me offer you my definition of social justice: I keep what I earn and you keep what you earn. Do you disagree? Well then tell me how much of what I earn belongs to you–and why?"

It is wrong for the government to force people to support welfare by force. If we allow it to do so, we may find that force being used in ways we never imagined. Any society built upon the idea that the needs of the many out way the rights of the individual will at some point come to calamity. It is only by securing the rights of the individual that any rights at all are protected. If we protect the individual, we protect society.

By securing your right to your apple orchard (and the fruit of your labor), we are securing a peaceful society. The only other option is violence. And to quote Ayn Rand, "A gun is not an argument."

Furthermore, increased freedom leads to increased prosperity. For most of history, the mass of humanity lived in abject poverty. Then, starting around 200 years ago, wealth began to explode across the globe. What happened? There were many factors, but it was the widespread expansion of free market ideas that laid the groundwork.

For the first time in human history, a peasant could profit from his labor and make a name for himself. The competitive nature of the market made once expensive goods available to the common laborer. People were no longer under the rule of a feudal lord system. Democracies were holding their governments accountable. And people began generating wealth at an unprecedented rate.

Government did not cause this. Private industry did. The world has never seen the amount of wealth that humanity has today. For the first time in history, humanity has seen what life could be like without poverty.

People don't have to live in poverty. They could achieve something with their lives. The power of freedom changed the world.

At the same time, in their zeal, people began trying to speed up the process through government intervention. They attempted to create a utopia through the power of government. But only private industry and mutually beneficial trade creates wealth. Government can only assist by protecting the innocent and building infrastructure. It cannot create wealth. It can only move it around (i.e., take it from some and give it to others).

If we want people to prosper, even the poorest of the poor, we need to let freedom run its course. We cannot attempt to cut corners by stealing from some to give to others.

Chapter 8

THE LIE THAT HAS STOLEN OUR DESTINY

"The sacred rights of mankind... are written, as with a sunbeam, in the whole volume of human nature, by the hand of the divinity itself; and can never be erased or obscured by mortal power."

～ Alexander Hamilton ～

When we first hear these ideas, we might feel as though we have to choose between welfare or destitution. The fear is that once we remove the welfare safety net, we would force millions of families and elderly people onto the streets. The compassion in most people may cause them to ignore the objectionable nature of welfare so they can avoid such a tragedy.

Yet, this choice is known in the rules of logic as a "false dilemma." This occurs when you limit the available choices in an argument too much. You are forced to pick between A or B, when in fact there's an option C (and D, E, and F) as well. Opposing welfare does not mean we are advocating for poverty in its place. There are more options than welfare or destitution.

Today, there are tens of thousands of charities and non-profits doing amazing work to help the needy. Millions of people donate to them who want to see social statistics change. These charities are not just passing out food, clothing, and offering shelter to those most in need. Many of them are working with people to help them get on their feet and reach some sort of social stability.

If we removed the welfare net, hospitals would not turn people away en masse because they weren't insured. Children would not go uneducated by the millions without welfare checks. Humanity, though capable of committing great evil, is more disposed to incredible compassion. As an example, since its conception, the Catholic Church has opened and funded thousands of hospitals worldwide – all through donations. When faced with real need, humanity responds.

Furthermore, most metrics show that the poorest of the poor are wealthier than they have ever been in human history. Reports from the U.N., World Health Organization, and the C.D.C. support this conclusion.

This means that as the world gets wealthier, the need for welfare shrinks. Indur Goklany states that for the first one thousand years after Christ, most people lived on one dollar a day worldwide (in 2000 standard dollars). By the 1800s, that had grown to $650 a year (or $2 a day). By 2001 that had grown to $6,000 a year, which is a 923% increase. Every country has seen an explosive growth in individual wealth, not just the wealthy ones.[9]

Not only are the poor wealthier, but their money purchases more food than ever before. The price of food, once you take inflation into consideration, has dropped by 75%.[10] This means that people can buy more food with less money.

As the world grows in wealth, everyone benefits, not just the wealthy. As competition enters the market, prices for commodities go down. This means the poorest laborer is the one who benefits. He can now afford what was once only available to the rich.

At one point, only the wealthiest people could afford to travel by air, or buy a computer, or own a cell phone. Now, thanks to capitalism and free trade,

9. Goklany, 40-44.

10. Goklany, 26.

hundreds of millions of people have access to these things. Thus, as charities work with the poor, the poor have access to more wealth than they ever have before.

When it comes to government-run welfare, our choice is not between welfare and destitution. We do not have to let our compassion override justice. We can hold onto our high ideals of equality and work to bring the poorest of the poor out of poverty. They are not mutually exclusive.

Not only should we remove state run welfare, but we can do it without letting humanity fall into horrific poverty. We have to trust that people will still be human when a gun is no longer pointed at their heads. We must believe that people will be generous if there aren't whips at their backs. Basically, we must have more faith in good than evil.

Chapter 9

THE HUMAN RIGHT THAT DOESN'T EXIST

"I cannot undertake to lay my finger on that article of the Constitution which granted a right to Congress of expending, on objects of benevolence, the money of their constituents."

∾ James Madison ∾

Some argue that access to healthcare is a natural right, just as is your right to life, freedom, and wealth. This means the government should guarantee access to modern healthcare. Though we should commend these goals, one person's rights cannot violate those of another. Which, as we will see, means we cannot use the government to achieve these noble ends.

It is virtuous to want to give every individual access to modern healthcare. But when we use the coercive force of government to do it, we are violating one life for the sake of another.

Someone, somewhere must develop pharmaceutical drugs. Someone, somewhere must spend years in school to develop the skills necessary to perform surgery. In every medical procedure, someone, somewhere has to do something. That means that someone, somewhere has to be paid for their labor and service. Either that, or we have to force them to do it.

In a socialized healthcare system, the government pays doctors, nurses, chemists, and researchers. Their income comes from taxes. Thus, one person's medical service is paid for by taking money from someone else. If we say that healthcare is a natural right, then we are saying one person's rights justifies stealing from another.

But some might argue, "No, we're just saying that someone shouldn't die from cancer when someone else owns four yachts. If we do not tax the yacht owner, we are placing one life above another. We are saying that the wealthy person's luxury items are more important than another person's life. This is not just. The moral demands of justice require that we keep this from happening."

Though a compelling argument, it is flawed.

This argument assumes that a wealthy person is at fault for a poorer person's death (by not paying for their treatment). In this argument, he is a murderer. By the same logic, we should prosecute every wealthy person for murder because they did not pay for a poor person's medical bills who died from a treatable condition. Failure to give is not a crime. Theft, though, is.

Also, we are saying that one group of individuals has the right to decide when to overturn the inherent rights of others. We are saying that some people can tell others how to live. It may seem innocent and even right in one context, but this principle's moral foundation is akin to slavery and despotism.

The other option is not to tax people to pay for healthcare, but rather make doctors offer their services at a reasonable price. This argument states that doctors and pharmaceutical companies cannot refuse to treat people because they can't pay.

Again, this means that one person's need warrants enslaving others.

People go to school for years, and spend hundreds of thousands of dollars to become doctors. They spend years laboring to gain the skills and tools needed. What right do we have to their labor? Why do we have the right to tell them how much they can charge for their services?

Pharmaceutical companies spend millions on research and development. Without them, we wouldn't have the miracle medicines we do today. They owe us nothing. They have rendered a huge service to humanity. We do not have the right to tell them what they can and cannot do with that labor. They spent their lives in this effort. We have no right to their lives, nor the fruits of their labor.

Though we may like the idea of universal healthcare as an natural right, enacting it requires unethical means. We either must force medical professionals to serve everyone, or we must tax people to pay for these services. Both of these options are immoral.

Finally, capitalism has brought about greater access to medicine than ever before in history. Are people still dying from treatable diseases and disorders? Yes, but fewer than ever before (when looked at per capita).

Furthermore, there are more charities all over the world bringing medical access to more people. Diseases that once killed millions are now mere nuisances. Society is on an upward trend. As people become wealthier, access to medicine increases. Everyone benefits. Even if a new medicine or treatment is expensive when it first comes out, the market will force those prices down over time. Which will give more and more people access to them.

We do not have to choose between socialized medicine and rampant disease and death. Welfare does not generate wealth. It just moves it around. Without welfare and socialized medicine, access to healthcare will continue to rise worldwide. There is no shortage of generosity and desire to see these high ideals achieved. And we can do it without forcing people into "charity."

Chapter 10

OUR NATIONAL WEALTH PREVENTION POLICY

"Give me your tired, your poor,
  Your huddled masses yearning to breathe free,
  The wretched refuse of your teeming shore.
  Send these, the homeless, tempest-tossed, to
    me:
  I lift my lamp beside the golden door."

∾ Emma Lazarus ∾

The immigration problem in this country threatens the very core of who we are and the engine that has made us a great nation.

Some might be wondering why a discussion on immigration is included as part of this work. It is because a proper immigration policy is integral to a moral government.

The New Colossus

In B.C. 305, the ruler of Cyprus besieged the Greek City-State of Rhodes. He was attempting to gain a strategic military position in the Mediterranean. Rhodes was an influential City-State located on an island that held access to many parts of the Aegean Sea. Cyprus thought Rhodes would make a good military base. They blockaded the island for over a year to capture it, but failed to defeat the inhabitants. Cyprus eventually retreated.

To commemorate their victory, Rhodes built a statue known as the Colossus of Rhodes. It symbolized their military strength and fortitude against overwhelming odds. It was included as one of the Seven Wonders of the ancient world because it was one of the tallest structures in antiquity.

Architects from the 19th century based the Statue of Liberty on what they thought the Colossus would have looked like.

In her sonnet *The New Colossus*, Emma Lazarus immortalized the difference between the ancient Colossus and Lady Liberty:

"Not like the brazen giant of Greek fame,
With conquering limbs astride from land to land;
Here at our sea-washed, sunset gates shall stand

A mighty woman with a torch, whose flame
Is the imprisoned lightning, and her name
Mother of Exiles. From her beacon-hand
Glows world-wide welcome; her mild eyes
    command
The air-bridged harbor that twin cities frame.
'Keep, ancient lands, your storied pomp!' cries she
With silent lips. 'Give me your tired, your poor,
Your huddled masses yearning to breathe free,
The wretched refuse of your teeming shore.
Send these, the homeless, tempest-tossed to me,
I lift my lamp beside the golden door!'"

The latter part of this sonnet was inscribed onto the Statue of Liberty. Because of Emma Lazarus the Statue of Liberty no longer symbolized the military might of a powerful state. Instead, it became a welcoming beacon for anyone who hoped to build a new life.

It appears that Ms. Lazarus understood something that we sometimes forget. Humanity's default condition is not abject poverty.

When children come into this world, their spirits are not crushed and their hopes are not dashed. If allowed to flourish, they will seek to do something great with their lives. No little boy or girl dreams of being destitute.

People have to be beaten into poverty. And their

spirits have to be broken if they are to remain there. The world has to make people poor. Pain and suffering are not the baseline of human existence.

The belief that all people can better their lives is foundational to the principles of freedom. Even those who have been beaten and crushed into misery can be nurtured back into their original state if only given the chance. This is what Ms. Lazarus meant when she wrote her sonnet.

What other countries consider "wretched refuse," we believe have the capability of greatness. When other countries reject those in misery, we welcome them with arms wide open. We believe they can achieve something great. Lazarus recognized our destiny as the Mother of Exiles. Almost every person in this country came from those "huddled masses yearning to breathe free." And we have become the most powerful nation in the world. The world's tired, poor, and homeless created the most powerful country in history. That is what freedom can do.

Fear Chokes the Fire

When Lady Liberty began to symbolize the hope of a new life, our legislators began to institute immigration quotas. We call them quotas, but they are really limits. The first immigration quotas were based on racists notions. They stated that people from Eastern Europe were less intelligent than those from Western

---

The world's tired, poor, and homeless created the most powerful country in history – that is what freedom can do.

Europe. Thus we limited the number of Eastern European immigrants.

On one side you had Lady Liberty welcoming the "tempest-tossed" to a chance to build a new life. On the other side you had Americans afraid that immigrants would take away jobs and disrupt our culture. They feared that inferior Eastern European genes would mix with our pure American blood.

To this day, our immigration policy is based on the fear that immigrants will erode our culture and take jobs away from Americans. But history tells us that these fears are ungrounded.

For thousands of years superpowers have fought against the influx of immigrants for the same reasons. The Babylonians, Assyrians, Egyptians, Greeks, and Romans all fought against outsiders. They feared these groups would destroy their society. They built walls and fought wars to keep them out, and it never worked.[11]

But their societies did not change. We notice a difference in people's names, but the material culture wouldn't change. Also, never once did an immigrant group cause the downfall of a society. Superpowers generally cause their own collapse. To quote William Durrant: "A great civilization is not conquered from without until it has destroyed itself within."

When we look at the immigrant waves of the 19th and 20th centuries, we see the same thing. People brought over their languages and cultures. They tended to group together to maintain some sense of home. This led some Americans to believe that they were trying to transform our culture into theirs, but they weren't. They were just trying to adapt to life in a new world.

Trends show that by the second or third generations, immigrants begin to culturize. They speak our language, wear our clothes, and listen to our music. They become American. This is a natural process that has happened for thousands of years in all different

---

11. We need to secure our boarders. That is not in question. It is one of the delineated duties of the Federal government by the Constitution. But if it is easy for individuals to come to the land of opportunity, why would they need to sneak across the boarder? If everyone that wanted to come to our country could, and they had to go a background check, a reformed immigration policy would make our borders safer.

parts of the world. Most of the time the only thing that changes are people's last names.

Secondly, immigrants won't eat up our jobs. This fear comes from the idea that there is a limited amount of wealth in the world. Which means there is a finite number of jobs. This is a fallacy that has infected almost everyone in our country, and influences our immigration policy.

As we have already discussed, wealth is immaterial. We use a trade medium (money), but ultimately money has no value in and of itself. Wealth comes from people producing things of value. Wealth doesn't exist in the material world. It is not a finite resource. It is limitless.

This means that an influx of immigrants won't "take away from the rest of us." It may cause temporary disruptions in the market, but the market will stabilize.

Furthermore, individuals will rise up from within those communities to generate new wealth. Wealth we could not create without them. They will come up with new ideas and innovations that will bring more value to our society.

Money is not the source of our nation's wealth. People are. People that other countries consider "wretched refuse" and "homeless." Emma Lazarus saw that these people bring great possibilities to our country.

Will some choose to stay in poverty? Yes. But the human spirit is too resilient for that to be the default condition of all people. This is especially true if they transplant into a free society that believes all people are capable of greatness. Our immigration policy must change. Fear has guided it too long.

No Assistance Necessary

When Ms. Lazarus wrote this poem, she was not welcoming the poor of the world to come and live off of government welfare. At the turn of the century there were few (if any) social welfare programs available.

Ms. Lazarus was speaking of the immense opportunity a country like America had to offer. She was speaking of the profound ability that every human possesses to achieve greatness. If people are given the chance to be free and build their own life, they can, and will, pull themselves out of the mud.

People are capable of so much more than poverty. The homeless that Ms. Lazarus discussed do not need more money to fix their problems. They need hope. If someone has hope in their spirit, no circumstance can stop them from achieving what is in their heart.

The influx of people looking to build a better world is the life-blood of our society. It is what gives us strength. People come to this country because they want to produce wealth. That is what makes us so powerful and alluring. If we are to be the country we were meant to be, then we must address the problems

---

Money is not the source of our nation's wealth. People are.

---

in our immigration policy. Otherwise, Lady Liberty stands alone.

Let us once again be the country that claims the orphan as her child. Let us once again house the exile. Let us once again welcome the lost and comfort the oppressed.

We have nothing to fear and so much to gain. If they cannot come here, then where will they go?

Chapter 11

RISING FROM THE ASHES

"The time is near at hand which must determine
whether Americans are to be free men or slaves."

◇ George Washington ◇

The points raised in this book are challenging to
say the least. If captivated by them, we must ask a
pragmatic question: "Can this even work in the real
world? And if the answer is yes, then how do we
do it?"

The principles of freedom and individual rights can
exist in the real world. For the first half of our nation's
history they did. It has only been in the last century
that socialist and communist ideas have entered our
system of government.

The problem is not so much with the mechanics of a government based on individual rights, but rather our engrained perceptions of government.

Everyone alive today has been born into a world where the only government they've known is a blend of capitalism and socialism. Every experience with government involves, at some level, goverment intruding into the lives of individuals. This makes it difficult to imagine a world where this isn't the case. We cannot envision a world without state-run welfare or government intervention. It is normal for us. And these programs often seem to do good things for society. This makes it challenging to see how things could be different. But that does not mean it is impossible.

Let's look at the political circumstances of the 1860's to help illustrate. Looking back at the Civil War it is obvious to see that the pro-slavery South committed heinous human rights violations. But it was not so obvious to everyone at that time.

For centuries, Americans and Europeans believed that Africans were sub-human. It wasn't until the 19th century that this idea was seriously challenged. To the people living in the Southern States of America, slavery was normal. And their experiences often supported their prejudices. Africans were uneducated. They were dirty. They didn't live as long as white people. And even though all these perceived differences were caused by the fact they were slaves, many people couldn't see beyond their prejudice. In their perception of the world, Africans were not human. They were wrong, but they did not know it.

Furthermore, the Southern economy was built upon slavery. It has been estimated that the slave population of the South was worth more than the railroads, factories, and banks of the United States combined.

Put yourself into the shoes of an 1859 plantation owner. Slavery is all you have ever known. Your schools taught you that slaves weren't human. Your parents taught you that slaves weren't human. Your entire experience has shown you that slaves aren't as developed as whites. And the entire economy depends on slavery. For you, abolitionism would have been incomprehensible.

Abolishing slavery would have seemed like the end of the world. You would envision your economy grinding to a halt. Countless jobs would disappear. Tens of thousands, if not hundreds of thousands of people would end up on the streets. Trains would stop running. Farms would stop producing. Bank vaults would empty. Groceries and markets would close.

Because slavery was so intertwined into your world, it would have been almost impossible to see a world without slavery.

But the moral demands of justice required that slavery end. It didn't matter the side effects. If abolishing slavery cast the entire country into an economic maelstrom, so be it. Enslaving your fellow man is wrong on all accounts. And even though it took the South time to recover, the world did not end.

Today we live in a similar world. The government steals from some and gives to others on a regular basis. We have grown up in this system. It is normal and doesn't seem out of place. We have adopted mindsets and worldviews that make it okay and even admirable to do so. Many portions of our society heavily rely on government intervention for support. And many of these programs provide real benefits to people.

But slavery also provided real benefits to people as well. That didn't make it right.

For us, reforming the government based on individual rights seems like it could spell disaster.

Our economy might collapse. Countless jobs could disappear. Tens of thousands, if not hundreds of thousands of people might end up on the streets. An untold number of businesses could close.

Because the government is so enmeshed into our world, we cannot see a world without it.

But the moral demands of justice require that we find a way. Justice dictates that we stop robbing our fellow man to support the lives of others. Just as the world did not end with the abolishment of slavery, so the world will not end with the establishment of a government that protects individual rights.

We must come together–as our founding fathers did–and find a way to fashion our world according to the ideals of justice. It is not an easy problem to solve, but we are not starting from the beginning. We stand on the backs of giants and a strong foundation.

Below are seven questions to start that journey. If we can find answers to these questions, then we will be well on our way to a new and brighter world.

The Seven Strategic Quetsions:

1. Seeing that the Constitution has failed to accomplish its mission, can it be repaired and bolstered? Or does it need to be completely rewritten?

2. How will, we as a society, take care of the least amongst us without the help of government assistance programs?

3. How will we continue to fund medical and science research and development? Is there a way to fund these things through the government that doesn't violate the rights of all people?

4. What do these principles mean for things like public education and infrastructure (like interstates and sewer systems)? Can we honor the rights of individuals and still fund these things through the government?

5. Are there ways to keep beneficial programs like welfare and social security with an "opt-in" system? If so, how could that be implemented?

6. What other areas of our government have been influenced by socialist ideas? What sorts of regulations exists that are incongruent with inherent equality? How do these ideas affect regulatory entities (like the EPA, FCC, and the Federal Reserve)?

7. Can we continue to lead the world in innovation and breakthrough without government support? If so, how? If not, how can we modify what we're doing to be morally ethical?

These are not all the questions that need to be answered. But this should get us started.

These questions *have* answers, answers that honor the inherent rights of all individuals *and* benefit every person in our society. We must only find them.

This is why we must rally around the idea of inherent equality and pool our knowledge, experience, and wisdom. Only then can we build a government–and country–the likes of which the world has never seen.

One error into which many people fall is looking back rather than looking forward. There are many people who look back at our nations founding as the key to our future. We need to *study* our past to *inform* our future, but we must not *return* to the past in *place* of our future.

The United States may have operated from these principles before, but we live in a different world today.

We need to study the past to inform our future, but we must not return to the past in place of our future.

Our society functions in a very different manner than it did 250 years ago. We cannot look to the past for answers. The past can educate us and give us insight, but we must innovate for the world around us today. We must do what the founding fathers did, but for our time. We must dream up something the world has never seen before.

The founding fathers built what they did for the world in which they lived. We must do the same.

Our nation has a destiny. We were meant to be a shining light to the world. We were once known as the "Empire of Liberty." This is our heritage and our future.

We have already had a massive impact on the world around us. We have inspired many countries to adopt democracies and the basic tenets of individual rights. Thus, we have been responsible for untold millions experiencing new levels of freedom.

We have a mandate to return to our first love and once again lead the charge in freedom. The only question is, will we heed the call? Or will we pass the baton like so many before us?

May we ever lead the charge.

A CHRISTIAN DEFENSE OF
LIBERALISM

Appendix

A CHRISTIAN DEFENSE OF LIBERALISM

Jesus never spoke directly about politics. As Christians, this poses a problem because it leaves us without clear direction. How can we be sure Jesus would support this view of freedom? Would He allow people to do what they want? Or would he outlaw things like gay marriage, prostitution, drug use, etc.? Would He support public welfare and socialized medicine? Or would He tell us not to get involve and to "render unto Caesar what is Caesar's"? These are valid questions.

This could tempt us to ignore the political realm altogether. Since Jesus never spoke on it, maybe He didn't want us involved.

But there are a lot of subjects about which He never

spoke. For instance, parenting, marriage, business, science, etc.. Yet that doesn't stop us from extrapolating what His teachings meant for these areas.

We need to remember that Jesus said He had "many more things to say to us." And that He would "send the comforter (the Holy Spirit)" to lead us into all truth. So, even though Jesus never spoke on these topics, it doesn't mean He doesn't have an opinion on them.

Secondly, we shouldn't expect Jesus to discuss politics in the New Testament. It wouldn't have been relevant to the early church. The early church had no political power whatsoever, and was often persecuted by the government. How would a teaching on the proper role of government have helped them? It wouldn't have.

They needed teaching on what to do in a politically oppressive environment. They needed the answers to questions like, how do you deal with persecution? How do you hold onto your faith when you are dragged out of your home and publicly tortured? How are the promises of God still true when you, your friends, and your family are being martyred for your faith? These were the things that Christians of Jesus' day faced. So these were the issues He covered.

Furthermore, there are principles by which Jesus lived that can help us understand the role of government.

Biblical Foundations of Freedom

The Bible illustrates that we must let people choose for themselves how to live their own lives. We must ask, "How would Jesus respond to the gay marriage debate?" or "Would Jesus outlaw prostitution?" We can't know for sure, but scripture gives us a pretty good idea.

Jesus said, "And if anyone hears My words and does not believe, I do not judge him; for I did not come to judge the world but to save the world." (John 12:47). This is a startling verse that contradicts the worldview of many Christians. Many people expect Jesus to judge sinners for their lack of faith. Yet, Jesus states that He won't do that. At least not until the Day of Judgment.

How can we force our morality onto people and be like Jesus at the same time? Jesus did not say, "If people hear My words and do not believe, then form laws that force them to follow My teachings." Yet, this is what we are doing when we force our moral views onto others through legislation. We may not be saying, "You have to be Christian to be here," but that is in essence what we're doing when we force our morality onto them. If their actions do not violate those around them, how can we tell them how to live their lives? When did Jesus give us this authority? When did He ever model this behavior? Jesus always made it a choice to follow Him. Why should it be any different for us?

When the rich young ruler asked Jesus how to receive the Kingdom, Jesus told him what he must do. But the young man chose not to obey. Did Jesus force him to do it? No. Jesus recognized that people have free will and He never violated it. Jesus is our model. God calls us to imitate Him. How does forcing people to live by our values imitate Jesus?

Furthermore, Paul tells us never to judge the outside world for their beliefs and customs. He says, "What business is it of mine to judge those outside the church?" (I Corinthians 5:12). The bible does not give us permission to tell people how to live their lives. Instead, it commands us to be the salt and light of the earth. It tells us to be the aroma of Christ. But those things are supposed to attract people to us. The bible does not give us permission to force our worldview onto others.

This does not mean the church shouldn't evangelize. The church needs to be vigorous in its efforts to spread the good news of Jesus. But we shouldn't do this by legislating how people live their lives. Jesus ministered to everyone who asked for it, without regard to what they believed or their lifestyle. He always offered them love and the power to live a new life. We should do the same.

Money: The Root of All Good

Many people believe that "money is the root of all evil." But, as we have seen, this cannot be. Why then do people say this?

When people say "money is the root of all evil" they are misquoting 1 Timothy 6:10. It states, "the love of money produces all kinds of evil."

The Greek word we translate as the "love of money" means something akin to avarice or an intense jealousy.

Paul is referring to a form of greed that causes people to do evil things to gain material wealth. They do not wish to add value to the world by offering a product or service that others value. They lust for wealth with no understanding of where it comes.

This can lead to all sorts of problems. It can cause you to lie, cheat, steal, and harm your fellow man to gain wealth. This is evil.

Paul is referring to people who are willing to do evil things to obtain material possessions. He is not referring to individuals who work to produce something of value.

We must also remember the world in which the early church lived. A free system of trade did not exist. Some trading occurred, but most wealthy people got their money through slave labor or conquest. It wasn't until the last two hundred years that we began to adopt a system of free trade.

This may seem odd to us today because commerce is common. But five hundred years ago people did not have the social mobility we do today. Before this, wealth was locked up in some sort of aristocracy or feudal system. You were wealthy because you were born into it. Or because you had favor with a king or ruler. And they often got their money from slave labor, conquest, or taxation.

In the ancient world, it is easy to see why Paul would say that the "love of money produces all kinds of evil." If the only way you could become wealthy was through theft, deceit, slave labor, or conquest, then pursuing wealth would have been an evil ambition.

But today, the system of free trade allows people to trade their products and services with each other, value for value. There is nothing evil about that.

All of this to say, money in itself is not evil. Nor is wanting money. It means that you want to do something that society values. Today, wealth represents your impact on the world. It is a measurement of your hard work and the wise stewardship of that work.

In a very real way, because of capitalism, the love of money now produces all kinds of good.

Render Unto Caesar

Many Christians can revert to the adage, "render unto Caesar what is Caesar's, and unto God what is God's." They use this quote to illustrate how we should leave government alone and not worry ourselves with it.

Nowhere in this book are we asking people to defy the government by not paying taxes. This book was intended to educate people so that we could change our government into what it was meant to be.

But since the tax question comes up so often, let's look at what Jesus might have meant by that statement:

> Then they sent to Him some of the Pharisees and the Herodians, to catch Him in [His] words.

> When they had come, they said to Him, "Teacher, we know that You are true, and care about no one; for You do not regard the person of men, but teach the way of God in truth. Is it lawful to pay taxes to Caesar, or not?

> "Shall we pay, or shall we not pay?" But He, knowing their hypocrisy, said to them, "Why do you test Me? Bring Me a denarius that I may see it."

> So they brought [it]. And He said to them, "Whose image and inscription [is] this?" They said to Him, "Caesar's."

And Jesus answered and said to them, "Render to Caesar the things that are Caesar's, and to God the things that are God's." And they marveled at Him.[12]

This was not a direct question about taxes. It was a trap meant to imprison Jesus.

As the Messiah, the Jews expected Jesus to raise an army and overthrow Rome. If He said that they should pay taxes, it would undermine his assumed political ambitions. It may have also turned His followers against Him (especially the zealots). And if He said they shouldn't pay taxes, then they could report Him to the authorities as an instigator of hostility towards Roman rule. His response was brilliant. It evaded their trap by making it irrelevant.

Secondly, we need to remember that Jesus was writing to people who had no political power. And they would soon be under the government's oppression. He was not endorsing political abdication, nor was He endorsing a welfare state.

Today, we live in a representative government. The ideals of God-given equality form its base. This means we should influence government. This is a new world. Mark 12:14-17 does not give us the freedom to ignore political issues and let the government do what it pleases. We have a responsibility to do what is right.

---

12. Mark 12:14-17, NKJV

Welfare

When it comes to welfare, the same principles apply. God never gave us the right to take the property of another to help the less fortunate.

No matter how noble our intent, or successful the outcome, we cannot justify stealing from one to advance another.

Jesus did not force the rich young ruler to give up his goods to the poor. He made it an option for him.

Jesus never told His disciples, "Give to the poor, and if you do not have enough money to do it yourself, take it by force from others." The church should help the poor. But it cannot use the government in doing it.

"Plead the Cause of the Poor"

There are many places in the bible that discuss "pleading the cause of the poor" or "judging the poor with justice." Many have used these passages to support welfare policies. They cause some to think that social welfare programs are biblical.

These passages in scripture were written in a culture where the rich looked down on the poor. Rulers would not give them the same level of justice as the wealthy. And the wealthy would often enslave them. Much of the ancient world saw poverty as a curse from the gods.

Scripture is countering that mindset. It commanded the rich to treat the poor as human beings. These verses demanded that the wealthy uphold the rights of the poor. Ultimately, it is a defense of the inherent rights of all people.

It speaks nothing of state-run welfare.

Conclusion

Though Jesus never directly spoke on politics, His life can tell us a lot. He always gave people a choice to follow Him and His teachings. If we are to imitate Him in our lives, then we cannot force people to live by our morality. We must protect everyone's right to choose how they wish to live their own lives. We must respect God's lordship over their lives and renounce ours. When a moral government protects a free society, then the Church can flourish. It can seek to reveal the light. It can allow people to choose to follow Christ's teachings. In short, Classical Liberalism is very Christian.

AMERICAN
RESURRECTION

Here's a Preview of Another
Book by Sean,
The End of Days....

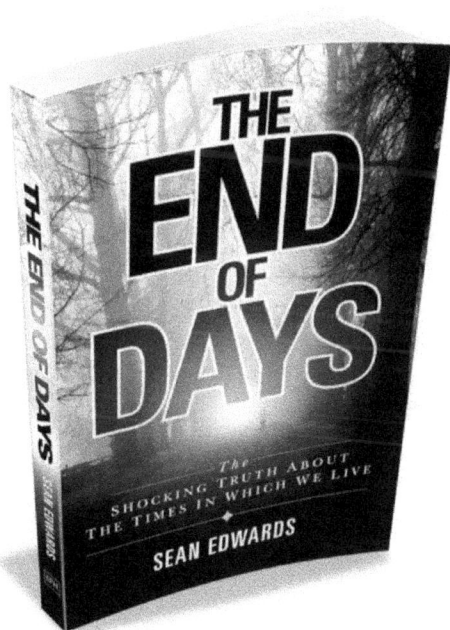

Chapter 1

THE END OF DAYS

"For unto us a Child is born,

Unto us a Son is given;

And the government will be upon His shoulder...

Of the increase of His government and peace

There will be no end"–Isaiah 9:6-7

The world appears to be in a state of constant deterioration and turmoil. Earthquakes, hurricanes, and wars all seem to prove that the world is moving towards a cataclysmic end. News outlets bombard us with disasters, murders, and rapes. Peace in the Middle East seems more impossible than ever. The number of countries with nuclear weapons has grown. The threat of a global economic meltdown seems ever more likely.

Should these events surprise the Church? These events appear to fulfill prophetic scriptures about the end of the world. For many, current events prove that we live in the last days. These people are certain that the Antichrist is right around the corner. They also believe that God will soon rapture us away. Passages in Revelation, Daniel, and other biblical books appear to describe these times. But is this true? Does scripture tell us that the end of the world is right around the corner?

Apocalyptic teachings on the end of the world have exploded in the last two hundred years. Many Christians expect to see the demise of civilization. Thousands of sermons, books, and teachings tell us that the Bible predicts this demise.

But what if it isn't true? What if there is another way to look at scripture that paints a different picture? One that also holds to traditional Christian ideas?

Most people refer to this view of the end times as "futurism." We call it futurism because it states that all the apocalyptic scriptures refer to events in our future. Futurism permeates our culture through movies, books, and TV shows. We have a fascination with the end of the world.

Yet many bible-believing scholars are not futurists.[13] And futurism has not been the dominant view of the end times for most of church history. The modern form of futurism, also known as "Dispensationalism," is only two hundred years old.[14] Concepts like the tribulation, Antichrist, and rapture did not exist for most of Church history. Most understood that the apocalyptic passages referred to the destruction of Jerusalem in A.D. 70.

For someone raised with a futurist worldview, this seems inconceivable. How could the end of the world have occurred two thousand years ago? The purpose of this book is to answer that question.

Concepts like the tribulation, Antichrist, and rapture did not exist for most of Church history.

But for now, let us examine the significance of our end times perspective. Our view of the end times affects every aspect of our lives. It impacts the way

---

13. Marvin Pate and others, *Four Views on the Book of Revelation* (Grand Rapids, MI: Zondervan, 1998), 17-18.

14. Clarence B. Bass, *Backgrounds to Dispensationalism* (Eugene, OR: Wipf and Stock Publishers, 2005), 64.

we see God. It affects the way we see ourselves. It defines our purpose. Since our view of the end times influences so much of our lives, we need to be willing to make sure we are right.

No one polishes brass on a sinking ship. If we believe that the world will end in fiery judgment, we will make no effort to improve it. This is why many Christians are not worried about the planet and the environment. Since the world is going to burn anyway, it doesn't matter what we do to it. What if we're wrong? What if we're supposed to be stewarding the land, making it better?

In the 1970s, Christians dropped out of college at a staggering rate. They felt that school was a waste of time because they believed the world was about to end. They wanted to spend their last days evangelizing the world to save as many souls as possible.

This was a great heart – but they were wrong. The world didn't end. The result was that non-believers completed their education and took professional jobs. Most of which many Christians were not qualified to fill. The church abdicated its position of influence because it believed "the end was nigh."

Where would we be today if they hadn't dropped out of college? What would our movie industry be like? What would our courts look like? How would the business world function? We will never know because well-intentioned Christians had a wrong view of the end times.

The course of human history can be changed by what we believe about the end of the world. This means that we must be certain we are right. We can't afford to be wrong.

Eschatology, or the study of the end times, is a fascinating subject. There are as many ways to interpret scripture as there are stars in the sky. But most interpretations fall into four eschatological categories: Futurism, preterism, idealism, and progressive dispensationalism.

Futurism holds to traditional apocalyptic views. It states that all the apocalyptic passages refer to events in our future.

Preterism believes the apocalyptic passages refer to events in our past. Primarily, the destruction of Jerusalem.

Idealism understands Revelation to be a metaphorical image that comforts Christians in distress. It does not believe that the book of Revelation depicts literal events. But rather these images communicate that Jesus is still King in all situations.

Progressive Dispensationalism is stuck between futurism and preterism. It holds that "end times" passages have many fulfillments. It can accept preterist and futurist arguments.

In this book we are going to look at preterism and futurism. We will challenge the dominant understanding of the "end of the world" in the Church. We will see that the enemy has deceived the Church into abdicating the future to evil. When we apply proper biblical and historical study tools to scripture, we will see that the world will not "end." There won't be an Antichrist or a Great Tribulation. The Church has missed her assignment. God called her to spread the gospel and redeem the planet, not to announce its end.

A Doctrine of Demons

There is strong scriptural and historical evidence to show that futurism is flawed. Not only that, but it enables evil to prevail upon the earth.

Futurism misrepresents God as an angry Father. Yet scripture says He is love (1 Jn. 4:16).

Futurism portrays the world as an evil place in need of judgment, but Jesus said He did not come to judge the world, but to save it (Jn. 3:17).

Futurism anticipates evil to expand in the world, when scripture says that we are to destroy the works of the devil (1 Jn. 3:8).

Futurism breeds anxiety and fear, when scripture says that God did not give us a spirit of fear (2 Tim. 1:7).

Futurism believes Satan still has power, yet Jesus disempowered him two thousand years ago (Col. 2:15).

Finally, futurism presents an inaccurate description of objective reality. It states that the world is getting worse, but it isn't. By most metrics, the world is getting better. People are living longer, healthier, and wealthier lives than ever before.

Also, the Church is growing at a rapid rate. It is not

By most metrics, the world is getting better. People are living longer, healthier, and wealthier lives than ever before.

---

on the defense. Futurism has blinded millions from stepping into their God-given destinies.

To prove this, we will go through most of the scriptures that deal with the end times and offer an alternative interpretation. We will see that there is a strong argument for the preterist understanding of the end times. We will see that there won't be an Antichrist or a tribulation in our future. We will discuss things like:

- The Antichrist
- The Great Tribulation
- The Rapture
- Matthew 24
- The Prophesies of Daniel
- The Book of Revelation

We will discuss their misinterpretation and how to look at them in a new way. It is the purpose of this book to show that the Bible does not predict armageddon. But instead it anticipates an improving world until it is completely redeemed.

Titus Flavius Josephus

We will be using Titus Flavius Josephus as one of our primary sources. Josephus is important because he was an eyewitness to the Roman conquest of Jerusalem in the first century. Secular historians have used his writings for centuries as reliable historical documents. Though, like any other historical documents, we do need to take some of his comments with a grain of salt.

He was a Jew by birth and lived from A.D. 37 to A.D. 100. He fought against Rome as a Jewish general at the beginning of the war. But Rome captured him at Jotapata. The Romans then drafted him to be an intermediary for them and the Jews.

The *Wars of the Jews* (known as '*Wars*' in short) is a detailed eyewitness account of the first Jewish War (A.D. 66–A.D. 70).

Josephus was not a Christian. But his writings appear to describe events predicted in the Book of Revelation and Matthew 24. Because of his unique perspective, Josephus will be a prominent person in this book.[15]

This Changes Everything

The ideas held in this book have the potential to transform your life, your church's life, and the course of history. When we understand that God is not coming to destroy the planet, but rather to redeem it, it changes our entire outlook on life.

There is an amazing saga unfolding around us: the complete redemption of human history.

Ultimately, we need to redefine the term "eschatology." Gordon Fee, in his work *Paul, the Spirit, and the People of God*, argues that Christians should be

---

15. Flavius Josephus, *The Works of Josephus: Complete and Unabridged*, trans. William Whiston (Peabody, MA: Hendrickson Publishers, Inc., 1987), ix.

an eschatological people. Meaning that Christians, through the Spirit, should bring the future (eternity) into the here and now. When people see Spirit-empowered Christians, they should see what eternity will look like.[16] Eschatology, then, should not be a study of the end of the world. But rather it should be the study of the beginning of a new one. Eschatology is the key to understanding who we are today and what we're supposed to be doing.

Eschatology is not the study of the end times. It is the study of our times.

Check Out:
The End of Days: The Shocking Truth About The Times In Which We live
on Amazon.com

---

16. Gordon Fee, *Paul, the Spirit, and the People of God* (Peabody, MA: 1996) 49-64, 124, 177.

Other Books by Sean Edwards:

The End of Days:
The Shocking Truth About The Times In Which We Live

Gay Marriage:
Why Conservative Christians Need To Support It

We Are The Danger:
A Christians Call To End The War On Drugs

Available on Amazon.com

How to Contact Sean

For more information on keynotes, workshops, and speaking engagements, contact Sean at:

Phone: (509) 624–2220
Email: info@SeanEdwards.com
Online: www.SeanEdwards.com

Sign up for Sean's Email Newsletter at:

www.SeanEdwards.com

To purchase bulk copies of this book at a discount for your customers, or for your organization, please contact Sean Edwards at:

info@SeanEdwards.com